WWII Ships, Vessels & Their Namesakes

of Savannah, Georgia

Breya Warnstaff

WWII Ships, Vessels and Their Namesakes of Savannah, Georgia
Copyright © 2023 by Breya Warnstaff, AncestorTracer Genealogy Services

All rights reserved. No part of this book may be reproduced or transmitted in any form or by any means without written permission from the author.

ISBN (9798863535357)

Printed in USA by AncestorTracer Genealogy Services

Dedication

I dedicate this to my relatives who served the military during WWII.
LEST WE FORGET.

PFC Jack Baldwin, Jr, US Marine, Iwo Jima
Maj James Thomas Beck, US Air Force
CPL Edward Dean "Bud" Brooks, Sr, US Army, Medical Unit
PVT William "Bill" Barney Brooks, US Army, 116 Inf Reg, 29 Inf Div, KIA
Sgt Ray S. Bunger, US Air Force
John William Cassabaum, US Navy, Naval Air Instructor, KIA
1LT Benjamin Hezekia Coe, Jr. US Air Force, Bombardier, Purple Heart
CPL Howard G Flanagan, US Army, 77th DIV, Pacific Theater
Sgt Perry Edward Hilleary, Sr. US Army, Radio Announcer
PFC Jesse Henry "Casey" Liggett, US Army, Purple Heart
PVT Bernard Paul Lindsay, US Coast Guard
CPL Donald Boyd "Darb" McBrayer, US Army, 7th Army
LTC Eldon Ellis "Mac" McBrayer, US Army, Korea
PFG George Lincoln McBrayer, US Army, Medic, Purple Heart
2LT James Nelson McBrayer, US Army, 577th Bomber Squadron
Brig Gen Madison Miller McBrayer, US Air Force
PFC William G McBrayer, US Army, 378th INF DIV, KIA
1LT Carl William Morey, Jr, DFC AM
SSGT Michael Redwine Rakestraw, Jr, US Army, HS CO 536 Amph Trac BN
CDR Allen Russell Rogers, US Navy, Distinguished Flying Cross
CPL Dewey Lee Spruill, US Army Phillipines
SSGT Grove Cleveland Suggs, US Army, 548 MIL Police
PVT Roy Edwin Toborg, US Army, BTRY C, II Coast ARTY
PVT Eugene James Tyler, US Army, 36th INF
QM3C Allison Dean Warnstaff, US Navy, USS Red Oak Victory AK-235
LT Charles Lee Warnstaff, US Navy, V-5 Aviation, Pilot
TSGT Frederick Irvin Wheeler, Jr. US Air Force
SM3 Alvin Hope Wheeler, Jr. US Navy
PFC James Shirley Leslie White, US Army, 498 Med Coll Co
MSGT Allen Russell Winder, US Army Corp, Honolulu
RM3c Donald Wornstaff, US Navy, USS Wright
F1C John William "Bill" Wornstaff, Jr., US Navy, USS Landing Ship Tank 1027
PVT Stanley Joseph Wornstaff, Army Air Corps Reserves, Vietnam

Table of Contents

WWII Ships, Vessels & Their Namesakes............1
of Savannah, Georgia............1
Dedication............3
Introduction............8
Liberty Ships............9
SS A Frank Lever............10
SS A. Mitchell Palmer............11
SS Addie Bagley Daniels............12
SS Alexander R. Shepherd............13
SS Andrew Pickens............14
SS Arlie Clark............15
SS Ben Robertson............16
SS Ben A Ruffin............17
SS Benjamin Brown French............17
SS Button Gwinnett............18
SS Casimir Pulaski............18
SS Charles H Herty............19
SS Charles C Jones............19
SS Charles A Keffer............19
SS Clark Howell............20
SS Crawford W Long............21
SS Dudley M Hughes............21
SS Earl Layman............22
SS Edward J Berwind............22
SS Edwin L Godkin............23
SS Felix Grundy............23
SS Florence Martus............24
SS Floyd Gibbons............24
SS Francis S Bartow............25
SS Frank P Walsh............25
SS George Handley............26
SS George Walton............27
SS George Whitefield............28
SS Hamlin Garland............29
SS Harry L Glucksman............30
SS Harry Kirby............31
SS Hoke Smith............32
SS Isaac S Hopkins............33
SS Jacob Sloat Fassett............33

WWII Ships, Vessels & Their Namesakes of Savannah, Georgia

SS James H. Couper...34
SS James Jackson..35
SS James Oglethorpe...36
SS James H Price...36
SS James Swan..37
SS Jerome K Jones...38
SS John C Breckinridge...39
SS John P Harris..40
SS John Milledge...41
SS John E Sweet..41
SS John A Treutlen..42
SS John E Ward...42
SS Jonas Lie...43
SS Joseph E Brown..44
SS Joseph H Habersham..44
SS Joseph H Martin...45
SS Joseph S McDonagh...45
SS Joseph Murgas..46
SS Josiah Cohen...46
SS Josiah Tattnall...47
SS Juliette Low..48
SS Langdon Cheves...49
SS Louis A Godey..49
SS Lyman Hall...50
SS Mack Bruton Bryan..50
SS Martha Berry..51
SS Milton J Foreman...52
SS Moina Michael..53
SS Nicholas Herkimer..53
SS Richard Coulter..54
SS Richard Upjohn..54
SS Risden Tyler Bennett..55
SS Robert Fechner...55
SS Robert M T Hunter...56
SS Robert Parrot..56
SS Robert Toombs...57
SS Ruben Dario..58
SS Rudolph Kauffmann...59
SS SamCebu...59
SS SamDart..60
SS SamHorn...60

WWII Ships, Vessels & Their Namesakes of Savannah, Georgia

SS Samuel T Darling ... 60
SS Stephen Leacock ... 61
SS Thomas W Murray ... 62
SS Thomas Wolfe ... 63
SS William H Edwards ... 63
SS William LeRoy Gable ... 64
SS William Terry Howell ... 64
SS William D Hoxie ... 65
SS William G Lee ... 65
SS William L McLean ... 66
SS William W Seaton ... 67
SS William L Yancey ... 68
SS William Black Yates ... 69
Coastal Cargo Ships 1945 ... 70
AV-1 Check Knot ... 70
AV-2 Becket Bend ... 71
AV-3 Flemish Knot ... 71
AV-4 Snakehead ... 72
AV-5 Link Splice ... 72
AV-6 Diamond Hitch ... 72
AV-7 Persian Knot ... 72
AV-8 Marline Bend ... 73
AV-9 Ring Hitch ... 73
AV-10 Grass Knot ... 73
AV-11 Sailmaker's Splice ... 74
AV-12 Long Eye ... 74
AV-13 Crossing Knot ... 74
AV-14 Solid Sinnet ... 75
AV-15 Flat Knot ... 75
AV-16 Horseshoe Splice ... 75
AV-17 Double Loop ... 76
AV-18 Half Knot ... 76
Naval Vessels 1942-1946 ... 77
USS Gazelle ... 77
USS Gorgon ... 78
USS Grecian ... 78
USS Implicit ... 78
USS Improve ... 79
USS Incessant ... 80
USS Incredible ... 81
USS Indicative ... 81

WWII Ships, Vessels & Their Namesakes of Savannah, Georgia

USS Inflict 82
USS Instill 83
USS Intrigue 84
USS Invade 84
USS Kittiwake 85
USS Magic 86
USS Minivet 86
USS Murrelet 87
USS Peregrine 88
USS Petrel 89
USS Pigeon 90
USS Pochard 91
USS Ptarmigan 92
USS Pylades 93
USS Quail 93
USS Redstart 94
USS Sunbird 95
USS Symbol 96
USS Threat 97
USS Tide 98
USS Tringa 99
Concrete Barges 1943-1944 100
Concrete No. 6 100
Concrete No. 7 100
Concrete No. 8 100
Concrete No. 9 101
Concrete No. 10 101
Concrete No. 11 101
Concrete No. 12 101

WWII Ships, Vessels & Their Namesakes of Savannah, Georgia

Introduction

In World War II, 127 ships and barges were built in Savannah, Georgia between 1942-1944 by Southeastern Shipbuilding Corporation, Yard. This is a combination of 88 Liberty, 18 Coastal cargo, 28 Naval Vessels including minesweepers and submarine rescue ships, and 7 concrete barges. This publication lists details of the ship, whom it was named after, and a little biography of the person whom the ship was named after. The launches usually took place at midday.

Credit goes to the Savannah Morning News, Savannah Bull Street Library – Genealogy Room, the Digital Library of Georgia, Georgia Historic Newspapers, Georgia Historical Society, and the ProQuest Newsstand.

Phone: 469-573-3626
Email: heirtrackers@gmail.com
On-Line Chat: go to our website, **https://AncestorTracer.com**

WWII Ships, Vessels & Their Namesakes of Savannah, Georgia

Liberty Ships

Southeastern Shipbuilding Corporation of Savannah, Georgia produced EC2-S-C1 type Liberty ships for WWII. The Liberty ships were approximately 441 feet and 6 inches long and could travel at a top speed of 11.5 knots. The Liberty ships are equipped with turbines that give top speeds of 14-17 knots. Each vessel is about 7,176 dwt and 10,414 tons with a cargo capacity of 500,000 cubic feet, 425 feet long with a beam of 58 feet. The ships were equipped with triple expansion reciprocating engines, due to easy handling and easily repaired. A single propeller will develop 2,500 horsepower. For fuel, oil is used. A 5-inch gun will fit in the gun foundation aft.

Liberty Ship Profile

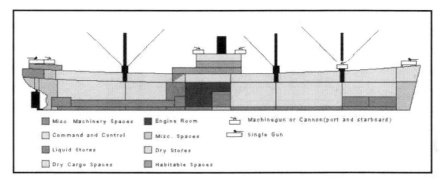

A typical Liberty Ship Profile

Typical Liberty Ship

SS A Frank Lever

The Hull #1072, SS A. Frank Lever was a Liberty cargo ship and launched on Monday, December 6, 1943. This ship was named after U.S. House of Representatives from South Carolina - Asbury Francis Lever (January 5, 1875 – April 28, 1940). U.S. House of Representatives from South Carolina. After the war, the ship was sold and renamed Brott and re-flagged for Norway in 1948. Then renamed again Finnborg for the Jorgen Krag company, Oslo in 1951. Sold to Liberian interests in 1954 and renamed Archanax. Sold again to Delta Marine Corp and renamed Mistral in 1967. She was scrapped in Taiwan in 1968 due to asbestos insulation.

SS A. Mitchell Palmer

The Hull #2436, SS Mitchell Palmer was a Liberty cargo ship and launched on Saturday, February 12, 1944. The ship was named after Alexander Mitchell Palmer (1872-1936), a Pennsylvania 26th Congressman and Attorney General. He was best known for overseeing the Palmer Raids 1919-1920 which violated the civil liberties of thousands of immigrants who were assumed to be anarchists or communists. The ship was operated by Isbrandtsen in 1947 and scrapped in 1967.

SS Addie Bagley Daniels

The Hull #2879, SS Addie Bagley Daniels was a Liberty cargo ship and launched on Thursday, September 28, 1944. This ship was named after Addie Worth Bagley Daniels (1869 – 1943), American suffragist leader and writer. She was married to Josephus Daniels, Secretary of the Navy. The ship was operated by States Marine as US Reserve fleet. She reefed off St. Catherine's Island, Georgia in 1975.

SS Alexander R. Shepherd

The Hull #2871, SS Alexander R Shepherd was a Liberty cargo ship and launched on Thursday, August 3, 1944. This ship was named after Alexander Robey "Boss Sheperd" Shepherd (1835-1902), who was the head of DB Board of Public Works. He was also listed in 3rd Battalion of the DC Columbia Volunteers, but was discharged after three months. He is also known as a controversial official, innovator, and governor of Washington, D.C. The ship was operated by Southeastern in 1944 and awarded to Northern Metal Co and scrapped in 1965.

SS Andrew Pickens

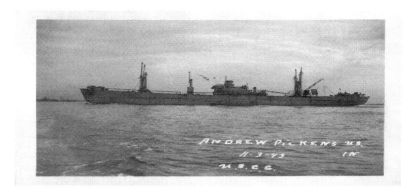

The Hull #1055, SS Andrew Pickens was a Liberty cargo ship and launched on Tuesday, July 20, 1943 and later operated by South Atlantic. This ship was named after South Carolina Congressman Andrew Pickens (September 13, 1739 – August 11, 1817). He was a militia leader in the American Revolution rising to rank of Brigadier General in South Carolina and a member of the US House of Representatives. The ship was later operated by South Atlantic in 1947 and scrapped in 1972.

SS Arlie Clark

The Hull #2897, SS Arlie Clark was a Liberty cargo ship and launched on Saturday, January 27, 1945. This ship was named after Arlie Clark (1919-1947). He was a soldier and served with the 1st BN, Winnipeg Grenadiers, A veteran of world war II, he was a prisoner-of-war at Hong Kong, returning to Canada in November, 1945. Rumor has it that he could have been chief engineer lost on the Hampton Roads, torpedoed by German U-106 on June 1, 1942 off Cuba, but no proof of it. The ship was used as a US reserve fleet, sold to Palmetto State from 1946-1955, Flomar 1955-1970 and then scrapped.

SS Ben Robertson

The Hull #2432, SS Ben Robertson was a Liberty cargo ship and launched on Tuesday, January 4, 1944. This ship was named after Clemson University and journalist Benjamin F. Robertson (1903-1943) who was a war correspondent, beginning in 1940 covering England for the NY paper. He was killed in a Pan Am airplane crash on February 22, 1943. The ship operated under A. H. Bull & CO of New York City through the end of the war. In 1947, it was sold to Constantine G. Gratsos Shipping Company of Athens. It was scrapped in Hirao, Japan in 1968 due to asbestos contamination.

SS Ben A Ruffin

The Hull #2442, SS Ben A Ruffin was a Liberty cargo ship and launched on Tuesday, April 11, 1944. The ship was named after Benjamin Allen Ruffin (1879-1939), the president of the first Lions Club International post in Virginia. 1928-1929. This ship was operated by Marine Transportation as the Wildcat in 1947 and scrapped in 1972.

SS Benjamin Brown French

The Hull #2867, SS Benjamin Brown French was a Liberty cargo ship and launched on Thursday, June 29, 1944. This ship was named after Benjamin Brown French (1800-1870), a politician and telegraph business leader, Clerk of US House of Representatives, Public Commission of Buildings in Washington, D.C. He was present at President Abraham Lincoln's inauguration and at the President's funeral. The ship was operated by Luckenbach, Pope & Talbot Inc in 1946; Dicman Wright & Pugh as a Reserve Fleet in 1948 and Northern Metal Company as scrap in 1967.

SS Button Gwinnett

The Hull #351, SS Button Gwinnett was a Liberty cargo ship and launched on Sunday, May 2, 1943. The ship was operated by South Atlantic. It was named Button Gwinnett (1735 – 1777), after a signer of the Declaration of Independence. He was born in Down Hatherley, county of Gloucestershire, Great Britain. He was a Representative of Georgia to the Continental Congress and a brief provisional president of Georgia in 1777. He was killed in a duel by rival Lachlan McIntosh following a dispute after a failed invasion of East Florida. The ship was operated by South Atlantic and scrapped in 1968.

SS Casimir Pulaski

The Hull #1053, SS Casimir Pulaski was a Liberty cargo ship and launched on Friday, June 25, 1943. This ship was operated by United Fruit after the war and named after General Kazimierz Pulaski (1745-1779), a Polish military commander recruited by Benjamin Franklin to join the American Revolution. He saved George Washington's life and co-founded the Army's Calvary Corp with Michael Kovats de Fabriczy. General Pulaski died leading combined American and French forces against the enemy in Savannah, Goergia. The ship was operated by United Fruit and scrapped in 1972.

SS Charles H Herty

The Hull #1069, SS Charles H Herty was a Liberty cargo ship and launched on Friday, November 5, 1943. This ship was named after chemist Charles H. Herty, Sr. (1867 – 1938). He created the first varsity football team at the University of Georgia. His chemistry revolutionized the turpentine industry. The ship was operated by the US Navigation and scrapped in 1967.

SS Charles C Jones

The Hull #1067, SS Charles C Jones was a Liberty cargo ship and launched on Friday, November 5, 1943. In 1946, the ship was declared a straggler. The ship was named after Charles Colcock Jones, Jr. (1831-1893), a Presbyterian minister, lawyer and mayor of Savannah, Georgia. This ship had two very near misses from bombs on June 15 and one soldier was slightly injured. The ship was operated by J. H. Winchester and scrapped in 1960.

SS Charles A Keffer

The Hull #2869, SS Charles A Keffer was a dry cargo Liberty ship and launched on Saturday, July 15, 1944. This ship was named after Charles Albert Keffer (1861-1935), a published Iowa horticulturist. The ship was operated by South Atlantic as a reserve fleet. The ship had a flash fire in deep tanks, on September 10, 1951 with loss of life and suffered slight structural damage due to an explosion while the vessel was moored in Philadelphia. The ship was scrapped in 1972.

SS Clark Howell

The Hull #2439, SS Clark Howell was a Liberty cargo ship and launched on Tuesday, March 14, 1944. After the war, the ship was sold privately in 1947 and scrapped in 1967. This ship was named after Clark Howell (1863 – 1936), a Pulitzer Prize winner. He was editorial executive and owner of the Atlanta Constitution. He also served three terms in the Georgia House of Representatives and was elected Georgia Senate in 1900. The ship was operated by Parry in 1947 and scrapped in 1967.

SS Crawford W Long

The Hull #349, SS Crawford W Long was a Liberty cargo ship and launched on Saturday, April 10, 1943. This ship was named after Georgia surgeon Crawford William Long (1815-1878). He was the first surgeon to use diethyl ether as an inhaled anesthesia working hospitals in New York City and Jefferson, Georgia. The ship was operated by International Freighting and scrapped in 1969.

SS Dudley M Hughes

The Hull # 1059, SS Dudley M Hughes was a Liberty cargo ship and launched on Friday, August 27, 1943. This ship was named after a Georgia Congressman Dudley Mays Hughes (1848 – 1927). He was elected Georgia Senate in 1882, a farmer and railroad executive. The ship was later operated by Grace Line in 1947 and renamed CATVAT scrapped in 1969.

SS Earl Layman

The Hull #2440, SS Earl Layman was a Liberty cargo ship and launched on Friday, March 17, 1944. This ship was named after Joseph Earl Layman (1912-1942), a Merchant Mariner 2nd Mate on the Stephen Hopkins, sunk and lost at sea on September 27, 1942. Layman was killed during the battle with the German commerce Raider Stiers and tender Tannenfels. The Liberty ship was operated by Polarus in 1947 and scrapped in 1967.

SS Edward J Berwind

The Hull #2891, SS Edward J Berwind was a Liberty cargo ship and launched on Saturday, December 16, 1944. This ship was named after Berwind-White Coal Mining Company founder, Edward Julius Berwind (June 17, 1848 – August 18, 1936). Born to German immigrants, he was appointed at the US Naval Academy at Annapolis, Maryland in 1864 by President Abraham Lincoln. The ship was operated by Wilmore and scrapped in 1961.

SS Edwin L Godkin

The Hull #1071, SS Edwin L Godkin was a Liberty cargo ship and launched on Tuesday, November 30 1943. This ship was named after Edwin Lawrence Godkin (1831 – 1902), an Irish born American journalist and editor of the New York Evening Post. He was born in Knckananna, Wicklow, Ireland. He studied law at Queens' College, Belfast and immigrated to the U.S. in 1856 and studied law under David Dudley Field in New York. The ship was operated by Luckenbach in 1947 and scrapped in 1971.

SS Felix Grundy

The Hull #352, SS Felix Grundy was a Liberty cargo ship and launched on Saturday, May 15, 1943. It was named after Felix Grundy (1775-1840), a Tennessee congressman and U.S. Attorney General. The ship was operated by South Atlantic and was scrapped in 1965 in New Orleans, Louisiana.

SS Florence Martus

The Hull #1068, SS Florence Martus was a Liberty cargo ship and launched on Thursday, November 11, 1943. The ship was named after Florence Martus (1868-1943), known as the "Waiving Girl" waiving at passing ships over 40 years in Savannah, Georgia. She was the younger sister and housekeeper of George W. Martus. The ship was operated by Polarus and scrapped in 1960.

SS Floyd Gibbons

The Hull #2875, SS Floyd Gibbons was a Liberty cargo ship and launched on Thursday, August 31, 1944 and was scrapped in 1966. This ship was named after Floyd Phillips Gibbons (1887–1939), a war correspondent for the Chicago Tribune. He reported during WWI and was one of radio's first news reporters and commentators. He was on the British steamer Laconia when it was torpedoed and lost an eye while in the battle at Belleau Wood. The ship was operated by South Atlantic and scrapped in 1966 in Kearny, New Jersey.

SS Francis S Bartow

The Hull #2447, SS Francis S Bartow was a Liberty cargo ship and launched on Monday, May 22, 1944. This ship was named after Brig. General Francis Stebbins Bartow, (1816-1861). He attended the University of Georgia and Yale Law School. He was one of the first martyrs for the Southern cause of the Civil War, being a member of the Whig and American parties. He was a Confederate hero, and died in Manassas battlefield, Virginia. . The 52nd Liberty Ship was christened by Miss Virginia Walton Purse, a past president of Winnie Davis Chapter, Children of the Confederacy. Mrs. Leon W. Johnson, served as matron of honor. The ship was sold privately in 1947 and scrapped in 1971.

SS Frank P Walsh

The Hull #2874, SS Frank P Walsh was a Liberty cargo ship and launched on Monday, August 28, 1944. This ship was named after Frank Patrick Walsh (1864 – 1939), an American lawyer. He stood for improved work conditions, better pay for workers and equal employment for all workers. He was also an Irish Nationalist. The ship was operated by R. A. Nichol in 1947, renamed Bluestar opeated by Traders SS; renamed Melody by Linares Cia Nav in Panama; it colladed and was damaged in 1956; then renamed Ikaros by Aldabi and then sold to Synthia Shipping Company in Panama and scrapped in 1966.

SS George Handley

The Hull #342, SS George Handley was a Liberty cargo ship and launched on Monday, December 7, 1942. This ship was named after the politician George Handley (February 9, 1752 – September 17, 1793), he was the 18th Governor of Georgia from 1788-1789. He was born in Sheffield, Yorkshire England and moved to Savannah in 1775. He served in the American Revolutionary War in the 1st Georgia Battalion and was a Freemason of Solomon's Lodge in Savannah. The ship was operated by Marine Transport and scrapped in 1964.

SS George Walton

The Hull #344, SS George Walton was a Liberty cargo ship and launched on Thursday, January 21, 1943. This ship was named after Sir George Walton (1664-1739), a signer of the Declaration of Independence and a representative of Georgia. During the American Revolutionary War, he served under General Robert Howe, receiving commission as Colonel of the First Georgia Regiment of Militia. He also served during the Battle of Savannah in 1778 led by Archibald Campbell in 1778. His political ally was Scottish General Lachlan McIntosh. He also served as a commissioner to negotiate with the Cherokee Indians in 1783. The ship was operated by Merchants & Miners and eventually burnt and sank in 1951.

SS George Whitefield

The Hull #1057, SS George Whitefield was a Liberty cargo ship and launched on Monday, August 9, 1943. This ship was named after George Whitefield (1714-1770) an English born preacher and co-founder of Methodism. The ship was sold to Norway and renamed Wilford 1947. Then sold to Italian owners in 1957 and then USSR in 1963 and scrapped in 1972.

SS Hamlin Garland

The Hull #1054, SS Hamlin Garland was a Liberty cargo ship and launched on Tuesday, July 6, 1943. This ship was named after Hamlin Garland (1860-1940), born in West Salem, Wisconsin. He was a lecturer and novelist. He is recognized for his work "A Son of the Middle Border" published in 1917. He won a Pulitzer Prize for best biography "A Daughter of the Middle Border" in 1921. Mrs. T. W. Langford had the honor of christening the ship with her maid of honor being Mrs. W. S. Fulghum. The ship was later operated by North Atlantic & Gulf and was scrapped in 1972.

SS Harry L Glucksman

The Hull #2445, SS Harry L Glucksman was a Liberty cargo ship and launched on Saturday, April 29, 1944. The ship was named after Harry L. Glucksman (1889-1938), an attorney who combined the Young Men's and Young Women's Hebrew Association into the Jewish Welfare Board in 1917. It was later renamed The Jewish Community Center. The ship was converted to a minesweeper (MSS-1) and operated by Merchants & Miners in 1966 and scrapped in 1973.

SS Harry Kirby

The Hull #2896, SS Harry Kirby was a Liberty cargo ship and launched on Saturday, January 20, 1945. The ship was named after Harry Kirby (1902-1942), 1st assistant engineer lost on the Lebore, torpedoed on June 14, 1942 by German U-172 off Panama. He was the only member of the crew to perish. The ship was sold privately after the war and then was scrapped in 1969.

SS Hoke Smith

The Hull #1061, SS Hoke Smith was a Liberty cargo ship and launched on Thursday, September 16, 1943 and later operated by American Export Lines. This ship was named after Michael Hoke Smith (1855-1931), who was a trial attorney and publisher of Atlanta Journal, a Georgia Governor and Senator, and Secretary of Interior. The ship was operated by American Export Lines by 1947 and scrapped in 1967.

SS Isaac S Hopkins

The Hull #2434, SS Isaac S Hopkins was a Liberty cargo ship and launched on Wednesday, January 26, 1944. The ship was named after Isaac Stiles Hopkins (1841-1914), a clergyman and first president of Georgia Institute of Technology. The ship was operated by Isbrandtsen and scrapped in 1961.

SS Jacob Sloat Fassett

The Hull #2863, SS Jacob Sloat Fassett was a Liberty cargo ship and launched on Wednesday, May 31, 1944. The ship was named after Jacob Sloat Fassett (1853-1924), a New York congressman from 1805-1911. The shipped was operated by Stockard and scrapped in 1965.

SS James H. Couper

The Hull #1063, SS James H Couper was a Liberty cargo ship and launched on Friday, October 1, 1943 and later operated by International Freighting. This ship was named after James Hamilton Couper (1794-1866), a Yale graduate and Georgia planter and slave owner, and having known for his advanced methods in farming. He was aboard the Pulaski steamer in 1838 when the boiler exploded and survived with 59 others. He planned the Church of Christ in Savannah, Georgia. The ship was used for Grain Program by International Freighting from 1948-1965, and then scrapped.

SS James Jackson

The Hull #343, SS James Jackson was a Liberty cargo ship and launched on Sunday, December 27, 1942. This ship was named after James Jackson (1757-1806), a Georgia politician. Born in Devonshire, England, he immigrated to Savannah, Georgia in 1772. During the Revolutionary War, he served in the 1st Brigade Georgia Militia, then the Battle of Cowpens and recaptured Augusta and Savannah. The ship was operated by South Atlantic and eventually scrapped in 1973.

SS James Oglethorpe

The Hull #341, SS James Oglethorpe was a Liberty cargo ship and launched on Friday, November 20, 1942. This ship was named after James Edward Oglethorpe (1696 – 1785), who founded and settled in Savannah, Georgia after being a British soldier. He was one of the first colonists. she was launched on 15 April 1945, sponsored by Mrs. Ellsworth Buck, wife of the New York Congressman; and commissioned at the Brooklyn Navy Yard, New York, on 6 June 1945. The ship was torpedoed by Capt. Walkerling (U-91) on March 15, 1943 and tried to make its way to St John in New Foundland, but was lost at sea with its Capt. Long, 30 merchant seaman, 11 Armed Guard sailors and 2 passengers.

SS James H Price

The Hull #2889, SS James H Price was a Liberty cargo ship and launched on Saturday, December 9, 1944. The ship was named after James Hubert Price (1878-1943), Virginia's New Deal governor, served in the Virginia House of Delegates. The ship was operated by Dichmann, Wright & Pugh and scrapped in 1964.

SS James Swan

The Hull #2872, SS James Swan was a Liberty cargo ship and launched on Saturday, August 12, 1944. The ship was named after James Swan (1754-1830), a Scottish patriot who participated in the Boston Tea Party, served at Bunker Hill, became successful in business, entered Massachusetts politics but became indebted and died in Paris after release from debtor's prison. The ship was operated by South Atlantic in 1947 and was wrecked by running aground and broken in two in 1952.

SS Jerome K Jones

The Hull # 1060, SS Jerome K Jones was a Liberty cargo ship and launched on Monday, September 6, 1943 and was later operated by South Atlantic. This ship was named after Jerome Kinsey Jones (1860-1940), a Georgia organized labor leader. He was an editor of Journal of Labor for 1898 until he died. The ship was operated by South Atlantic and scrapped in 1972.

SS John C Breckinridge

The Hull #350, SS John C Breckinridge was a Liberty cargo ship and launched on Thursday, April 22, 1943. This ship was named after Major General John Cabell Breckinridge (1821-1875), served as Confederate Secretary of War. Mrs. Arnold A. Wilcox christened the vessel as it was named after the lineal descendant of John Carson Breckinridge. Mrs. Charles S. Atwell, matron of honor, is the wife of the Vice President of Southeastern. It was the tenth cargo ship launched and manned by the Coast Guard. The ship was operated by J. H. Winchester and Wilmington Reserve Fleet and scrapped in 1965.

SS John P Harris

The Hull #2877, SS John P Harris was a Liberty cargo ship and launched on Wednesday, September 13, 1944. The ship was named after John Paul Harris (1873-1926), who was an entertainer promoted with Harris Comedy & Specialty Company, opening the first motion picture theatre in the world. He was also the 45th District Pennsylvania State Senate representative. The ship was operated by Black Diamond in 1947; renamed George M Culucundis by K&C in 1951; renamed Seavictor by Bournemouth SS Corp in 1952; renamed Evibell by Seacrest Shipping in 1954, sold to Bournemouth in 1957 and then to Doric Shipping in 1958; renamed Grethe by Bonamar Shipping in 1965 and scrapped in 1967 in Tsuneishi, Japan. .

SS John Milledge

The Hull # 346, SS John Milledge was a Liberty cargo ship and launched on Sunday, February 21, 1943. This ship was named after John Milledge (1757-1818), a Georgia Congressman and Governor. He fought in the American Revolution and took part in a raid of Savannah's royal armory to procure gunpowder and narrowly missed being hanged as a spy. He served as a colonel in the Georgia Militia. and then served as U.S. Representative, 26th Governor of Georgia and then U.S. Senator. He founded Athens, Georgia and the University of Georgia. The ship was operated by South Atlantic and scrapped in 1965.

SS John E Sweet

The Hull #2438, SS John E Sweet was a Liberty cargo ship and launched on Friday, March 3, 1944. The ship was named after John Edson Sweet (1832-1916), inventor of the first micrometer, designed and patented the upright steam engine, and made a governor for high-speed steam engines. The ship was operated by Black Diamond and was scrapped in 1965 in Philadelphia.

SS John A Treutlen

The Hull #2441, SS John A Treutlen was a Liberty cargo ship and launched on Monday, April 10, 1944. The ship was named after John Adam Treutlen (1734-1782), a first Constitutional Governor of Georgia. He was born Hans Adam Treuetlen in Germany. John was a Catholic who was prosecuted by the Protestant establishment He was murdered during an on-going political conflict of the colony. The ship was operated by South Atlantic, torpedoed in the English Channel in 1944, beached and scrapped.

SS John E Ward

The Hull #1070, SS John E Ward was a Liberty cargo ship and launched on Thursday, November 25, 1943. This ship was named after John Elliott Ward (1814-1902), a mayor of Savannah, Georgia and minister to China. The ship was used for Army Transportation Service, then operated by South Atlantic and scrapped in 1970 in Kearny, New Jersey.

SS Jonas Lie

The Hull #2876, SS Jonas Lie (aka Jones Lie) was a Liberty cargo ship and launched on Thursday, September 7, 1944. The ship was named after Jonas Lauritz Idemil Lie (1833-1908), a Norwegian-born painter of coastal and marine seascapes. The ship was sailed from Savannah, Georgia to New York, then to Liverpool where 25 sailors were paid off and Ricardo M. Garcia signed on along with 23 others. Capt. Von Schoen sailed from Federal Anchorage and it was torpedoed by a German U-1055 in the Bristol Channel and lost in 1945.

SS Joseph E Brown

The Hull #1057, SS Joseph E Brown was a Liberty cargo carrier ship and launched on Thursday, August 19, 1943. This ship was named for (1821-1894), Joseph Emerson Brown who served four terms as governor of Georgia during the War between the States. He served in the US State Senate in 1849, a judge of Blue Ridge Circuit in 1855, a governor of Georgia in 1857 and reelected in 1859, 1861, and 1863. After surrender of the state after the war, he was imprisoned, but was pardoned by President Johnson. He was Chief Justice in Georgia in 1868 and served as US Senator from 1880-1891. He died in Atlanta, Georgia on November 30, 1894. The ship was reefed off Panama City, Florida in 1977. Mrs. Thomas B. Fowler of Brooklyn, NY received the honor of cracking the champagne. Her matron of honor was Mrs. Edgar Hart of Statesboro, wife of Statesboro Chief of Police. Later the ship was operated by the Cosmopolitan and reefed 20 miles south-west of Destin, Florida in 1977.

SS Joseph H Habersham

The Hull #1064, SS Joseph H Habersham was a Liberty cargo ship and launched on Wednesday, October 6, 1943 and was named after Joseph H. Habersham (1751-1815), he was a Continental Army veteran, Georgia Congressman and 6th U.S. Postmaster General. The ship was later operated by Isthmian and scraped in 1961 in Tsuneishi, Japan.

SS Joseph H Martin

The Hull #1065, SS Joseph H Martin was a Liberty dry cargo ship and launched on Monday, October 18, 1943. This ship was named after Rev. Joseph H. Martin (1825-1883), pastor of 2nd Presbyterian Church in Knoxville, Tennessee. He was taken prisoner in 1863 by General Ambrose Burnside's Federals and the church was closed during the Civil War. The ship was sold to Dichman Wright & Pugh in 1948 as Reserve Fleet, then passed to Standard SS Co. LTD in 1949 and renamed "Christine" in 1950 and sold to Oceanways in 1950 and was scrapped in 1972 in Kearny, New Jersey.

SS Joseph S McDonagh

The Hull #2883, SS Joseph S McDonagh was a Liberty cargo ship and launched on Friday, October 27, 1944. The ship was named after Joseph Sylvester McDonagh (1879-1944), an electrician at the Brooklyn Navy Yard and secretary-treasurer of the American Federation of Labor Metal Trades Department. The ship was operated by Overlakes, wrecked and scrapped in 1946 at the mouth of River Canete, south of Cerro Azul.

SS Joseph Murgas

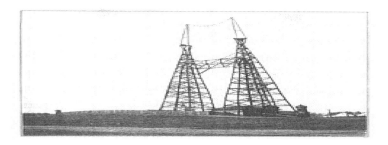

The Hull #2881, SS Joseph Murgas was a Liberty cargo ship and launched on Thursday, October 12, 1944. The ship was named after Jozef Murgas (1864-1929), a Slovak priest whose inventions contributed to amateur radio and wireless communications. The ship was operated by J. H. Winchester as a US Reserve fleet and scrapped in 1972 in Philadelphia.

SS Josiah Cohen

The Hull #2887, SS Josiah Cohen was a Liberty cargo ship and launched on Thursday, November 23, 1944. The ship was named after Josiah Cohen (1840-1930), a Pittsburgh attorney, judge, legal ethicist, and appointed judge of the Allegheny County, Pennsylvania orphan's court. He was born to a Jewish family in Cornwall, England and immigrated to the United States in 1857. This ship was operated by Overlakes in 1947; renamed Themoni by Kassos Shipping in 1947; operated by A. Frangistas and renamed Nicolaos Frangistas in 1964; renamed Kounistra by Kounistras Shipping in 1969 and scrapped in 1971 in Valencia.

SS Josiah Tattnall

The Hull #2884, SS Josiah Tattnall was a Liberty cargo ship and launched on Friday, November 3, 1944. The ship was named after Josiah Tattnall, III (1794-1871), son of Georgia senator and governor who served as commodore in the Navy during the War of 1812 and Confederate States Navy. The ship was operated by Wessell, Duval and scrapped in 1970 in Bilbao.

SS Juliette Low

The Hull #2446, SS Juliette Low was a Liberty cargo ship and launched on Friday, May 12, 1944. The ship was named after Juliette Magill Kinzie Gordon (1860-1927) who married William M. Low. She organized the first troop of the American Girl Guides in Savannah, Georgia, which was later known as The Girl Scouts. The ship was christened by Juliette's niece, Daisy Lawrence. The ship was used as US Reserve fleet, and later operated by South Atlantic and scrapped in 1972 in Brownsville, Texas.

SS Langdon Cheves

The Hull #1051, SS Langdon Cheves was a Liberty cargo ship and launched on Saturday, May 22, 1943. This ship was operated by AGWI Lines and named after Langdon Cheves (1776-1857), South Carolina congressman, attorney, judge, plantation owner, state legislator, U.S. Representative and president of the Bank of the United States. In 1811, Cheves was made Chairman of the Select Committee to look after Naval affairs. The ship was operated by AGWI Lines and scrapped in 1961 in Baltimore.

SS Louis A Godey

The Hull #1074, SS Louis A Godey was a Liberty cargo ship and launched on Monday, December 20, 1943. The ship was named after Louis Antoine Godey (1804-1878). His family were French immigrants who fled during the French Revolution. He was a newspaper editor, women's fashion magazine publisher and implemented a service to order copies of the magazines, an early version of mail order catalogs. Mrs. J. R. Wakeman had the honor to christen the ship. Mrs. Snyder Atwell served as matron of honor. The ship was renamed Samvannah by Anchor Line in 1943, scrapped in 1961 in Orange, Texas.

SS Lyman Hall

The Hull #345, SS Lyman Hall was a Liberty cargo ship and launched on Saturday, February 6, 1943. This ship was named after Lyman Hall (1724-1790). He served as representative of Continental Congress and Governor of Georgia in 1783-1784. He was one of three Georgians to sign the Declaration of Independence. He was also a pastor at Stratfield Parish in Bridgeport, Connecticut. The ship was operated by South Atlantic and scrapped in 1963 in Philadelphia.

SS Mack Bruton Bryan

The Hull #2893, SS Mack Bruton Bryan was a Liberty cargo ship and launched on Saturday, December 30, 1944. The ship was named after Mack Bruton Bryan (1907-1940), 3rd assistant engineer lost on the City of Rayville after hitting a German mine off Australia. The ship was operated by Merchants & Minters in 1947; renamed Transunion in 1951 by American Union Transport; renamed Jlan by Pacific Seafarers in 193; renamed Entella by Franklin Shipping in 1964; and scrapped in 1967 in Aioi, Japan.

SS Martha Berry

The Hull #2873, SS Martha Berry was a Liberty cargo ship and launched on Saturday, August 19, 1944. The ship was named after Martha McChesney Berry (1865-1942), who founded the Boys International School in 1902, Girls School in 1909 and Berry Junior College in Georgia in 1926. The ship was operated by Black Diamond as reserve fleet and scrapped in 1972 in Kearny, New Jersey.

SS Milton J Foreman

The Hull# 2882, SS Milton J Foreman was a Liberty cargo ship and launched on Saturday, October 21, 1944. The ship was named after Milton Joseph Foreman (1863-1935), an Army Lieutenant General, who served as Chief of Illinois National Guard, and national commander of the American Legion. The ship was operated by International Freighting in 1947; renamed Shinnecock Bay by Veritas Shipping in 1951; renamed Mount Shasta by Cargo & Tankships in 1960; renamed Shakara Jayanti by Jayanti Shipping in 1963; and scrapped in 1965 in Bombay.

SS Moina Michael

The Hull #2885, SS Moina Michael was a Liberty cargo ship and launched on Thursday, November 9, 1944. The ship was named after Moina Belle Michael (1869-1944), a professor at the University of Georgia, working with YWCA during World War I. She was known as the Poppy Lady, adapted from John McCrae's poem, In Flander's Fields', honoring support for veterans. The ship was operated by Stockard as US Reserve fleet and scrapped in 1971 in Panama City.

SS Nicholas Herkimer

The Hull #1052, SS Nicholas Herkimer was a Liberty cargo ship and launched on Tuesday, June 8, 1943. The ship was named after Nicholas Herkimer (1728-1777), a Revolutionary War military General, who was wounded at Oriskany and died from his wounds. This ship was operated by AGWI Lines and was scrapped in 1967 in Green Cove Springs, Florida.

SS Richard Coulter

The Hull #2878, SS Richard Coulter was a Liberty cargo ship and launched on Friday, September 22, 1944. The ship was named after Richard Coulter (1827-1908), a Pennsylvania banker, Union General, and member of the House of Representatives in Pennsylvania. He served during the Civil War as Colonel and commander of the 11th Pennsylvania Volunteer Infantry. The ship was operated by Overlakes and scrapped in 1960 in Baltimore, Maryland.

SS Richard Upjohn

The Hull #2864, SS Richard Upjohn was a Liberty cargo ship and launched on Thursday, June 8, 1944. The ship was named after Richard Upjohn (1802-1878), a noted architect of Gothic Revival churches. The ship was used in US Reserve Fleet, and then operated by T. J. Stevenson and was sunk as part of artificial reef program off Horn Island, Mississippi in 1976.

SS Risden Tyler Bennett

The Hull #2870, SS Risden Tyler Bennett was a Liberty cargo ship and launched on Saturday, July 22, 1944. This ship was named after Confederate Colonel Risden Tyler Bennett (1840-1913), was a distinguished Confederate officer and North Carolina congressman. Mrs. Mary Bennett Little had the honor to christen the ship named after her father. The matron of honor was Mrs. Kenneth Weeks and the maid of honor was Miss Sarah Dabney, Mrs. Little's granddaughter. This liberty ship was the sixtieth ship to be launched. The ship was operated by American West African Line and scrapped in 1963 in Philadelphia.

SS Robert Fechner

The Hull #1066, SS Robert Fechner was a Liberty cargo ship and launched on Thursday, October 28, 1943. This ship was named after Robert Fechner (1876-1939), who was a national labor union leader and director of the Civilian Conservation Corps. The ship was operated by South Atlantic in 1947; renamed Van der Waals by Netherlands Government in 1947; renamed Enggano by Nederland N. V. Stoom in 1950; renamed Amstellaan by Amsterdam N.V. In 1957; renamed Silver State by Pacific Overseas Naval Corp in 1961; and scrapped in 1967 in Taiwan.

SS Robert M T Hunter

The Hull #348, SS Robert M T Hunter was a Liberty cargo ship and launched on Sunday, March 28, 1943. This ship was named after Robert Mercer Taliaferro Hunter (1809-1887), who was a Georgia Congressman and Confederate States of America's Secretary of State. He served as Secretary of state of Confederacy following the resignation of Robert Toombs. He surrendered to federal authorities and was held prisoner for several months at Fort Pulaksi. Then he was Virginia Treasurer and died on July 18, 1887. It was the eighth vessel to be released. The christening honor of the ship went to Mrs. John L. Weeks with Mrs. Harry J. Fair, matron of honor. The ship was operated by the South Atlantic and scrapped in 1971 in Santander.

SS Robert Parrot

The Hull #2886, SS Robert Parrot was a Liberty cargo ship and launched on Thursday, November 16, 1944. The ship was named after Robert Parker Parrott (1804-1877), an artillery officer and foundry operator, who developed the Parrott Rifle. The ship was operated by Dichmann, Wright & Pugh, then Zidell Explorations, Inc. and scrapped in 1968 in Portland, Oregon.

SS Robert Toombs

The Hull # 347, SS Robert Toombs was a Liberty cargo ship and launched on Friday, March 19, 1943. This ship was named for Robert "Bob" Augustus Toombs, Jr. (1810-1885), a soldier and statesmen of Colonial period fame, a lawyer and politician and Georgia congressman and governor. He attended the University of Georgia (but was expelled in his senior year due to many infractions), then graduated from Union College of New York in 1828. He then studied law at the University of Virginia and admitted to Georgia bar in 1830. He was a 6' tall, over 200 lbs. gentleman. When the formation of the Confederacy found him among its leaders as secretary of state, he took arms as Brigadier General. At the end of the war, he was arrested and fled to Cuba and Europe but came back to Georgia in 1867 and died on December 15, 1885. Miss Natalie Todd Smith, daughter of William H. Smith, president of the Southeastern, had the honor of christening the ship. Her maid of honor was Miss Julia Butler, daughter of Col. And Mrs. E. George Butler. The ship was operated by the South Atlantic, later renamed USS General LeRoy Eltinge and scrapped in 1959 in Baltimore, Maryland.

SS Ruben Dario

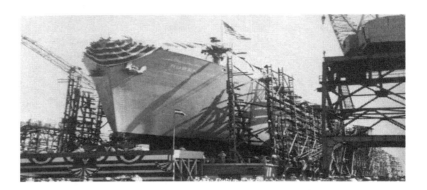

The Hull #2866, SS Ruben Dario was a Liberty cargo ship and launched on Thursday, June 22, 1944. The ship was named after Félix Rubén García Sarmiento (1867-1916), a Nicaraguan poet. The shipped was operated by International Freighting, and torpedoed by German U-825 on January 27, 1945, with no casualties and the ship was repaired and not scrapped until 1963 in Philadelphia.

SS Rudolph Kauffmann

The Hull #2888, SS Rudolph Kauffmann was a Liberty cargo ship and launched on Wednesday, November 29, 1944. The ship was named after Rudolph Max Kauffmann (1853-1927), a managing editor of the Washington Evening Star. The ship was operated by T. J. Stevenson as US Reserve fleet and scrapped in 1972 in Brownsville, Texas.

SS SamCebu

The Hull #2444, SS SamCebu was a Liberty cargo ship and launched on Sunday, April 23, 1944. The ship was built for the British Ministry of War Transport and later operated by the Bolton Steam Shipping company; renamed as Reynolds by Bolton Steam Shipping in 1947; renamed St Nicholas by Parana Cia de Vapores in 1951; renamed Panagos by San Ignatio Cia in 1956; renamed Amazon by Amazon Shipping in 1959; it was wrecked in 1963 in Spezia and scrapped as a total loss.

SS SamDart

The Hull #2437, SS SamDart was a Liberty cargo ship and launched on Wednesday, February 23, 1944. The ship was built for the British Ministry of War Transport, then operated by Mungo, Campbell & Co. She renamed Sedgepool by Pool Shipping in 1947; renamed Bobara by Tabor Shipping in 1954; renamed Flevariotissa by Marinos & Frangos in 1956; renamed Kapetan Andreas by Apiganos Corp in 1958; renamed Kitsa by Maractiva Cia Nav in 1965; and finally scrapped n Taiwan in 1967.

SS SamHorn

The Hull #2435, SS SamHorn was a Liberty cargo ship and launched on Saturday, February 5, 1944. The ship was built for the British Ministry of War Transport as MOWT, operated by Donaldson Bros & Black, and then scrapped in 1960 in Orange, Texas.

SS Samuel T Darling

The Hull #2433, SS Samuel T Darling was a Liberty cargo ship and launched on Tuesday, January 18, 1944. The ship was named after Samuel Taylor Darling (1872-1925), a medical expert on tropical diseases, pathologist and bacteriologist, and died in Beirut, Lebanon in a car accident. He received the Darling Foundation prize for malaria research. The ship was operated by Grace Line and scrapped in 1961 in Seattle, Washington.

SS Stephen Leacock

The Hull #2868, SS Stephen Leacock was a Liberty cargo ship and launched on Tuesday, June 11, 1944. The ship was named after Stephen P. H. Butler Leacock (1869-1944) a Canadian writer and humorist. Near the end of his life, the US comedian Jack Benny recounted how he had been introduced to Leacock's writing by Groucho Marx when they were both young vaudeville comedians. Benny acknowledged Leacock's influence and, fifty years after first reading him, still considered Leacock one of his favorite comic writers. The ship was operated by South Atlantic and scrapped in 1969 in New Orleans, Louisiana.

SS Thomas W Murray

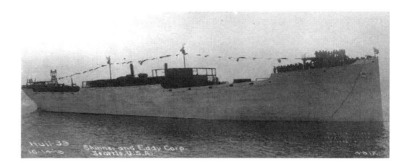

The Hull #2898, SS Thomas W Murray was a Liberty cargo ship and launched on Wednesday, January 31, 1945. This ship was named after Thomas William Murray (1889-1942), an English merchant marine, lost on the tanker William C. McTarnaban, torpedoed by German U-506 on May 16, 1942 in the Gulf of Mexico. The ship was operated by Cosmopolitan in 1947; renamed Seaglamour by Phoenix Shipping in 1951; renamed Barbara Michel by Southatlantic in 1954; renamed Ocean Alice, Pacific Isle; renamed Lisa B by Ventures Shipping in 1961; and renamed Grand Grace by Grace Navigation in 1964; and scrapped in 1968 in Taiwan

SS Thomas Wolfe

The Hull #1073, SS Thomas Wolfe was a Liberty cargo ship and launched on Wednesday, December 15, 1943. This ship was named after Thomas Clayton Wolfe (1900-1938), an author from North Carolina. The ship was used for United States Army Transportation, then operated by the South Atlantic and scrapped after 1965 in New Orleans, Louisiana.

SS William H Edwards

The Hull #2880, SS William H Edwards was a Liberty cargo ship and launched on Thursday, October 5, 1944. The ship was named after William Henry Edwards (1822-1909), a noted entomologist from West Virginia. The ship was operated by A. H. Bull and scrapped in 1967 in Portland, Oregon.

SS William LeRoy Gable

The Hull #2895, SS William LeRoy Gable was a Liberty cargo ship and launched on Saturday, January 13, 1945. This ship was named after William LeRoy Gable (1891-1942), who lost his life on May 25, 1942 when he served as Chief Engineer on the SS Carrabulle, was torpedoed and sunk by a torpedo from a German submarine U-106 and sunk off the Gulf of Mexico. Mr. Gable was declared Missing in Action. Mr. Gable had runaway to sea at the age of fourteen, and for thirty years served on the crew of SS Cassimir. Mrs. Florence M. Gable, the widow of William LeRoy Gable had the honor of christening the ship. The matron of honor was Mrs. L. S. Mason. The ship was renamed Cimon by Panama Shipping in 1947; renamed Archigetis by Sierra Cia. Navigation in 1955; renamed Western Venture by Pan Norse in 1960; sold to Wah Kwong in 1965; sold to Electra Carriers in 1968; and scrapped in 1969 in Taiwan.

SS William Terry Howell

The Hull #2894, SS William Terry Howell was a Liberty cargo ship and launched on Saturday, January 6, 1945. The ship was named after William Terry Howell (1917-1942), who lost his life on SS Carrabulle, was torpedoed and sunk by a torpedo from a German submarine U-106 and sunk off the Gulf of Mexico. The ship was operated by International Freighting; and scrapped in 1960 in Faslane.

SS William D Hoxie

The Hull #2443, SS William D Hoxie was a Liberty cargo ship and launched on Friday, April 14, 1944. The ship was named after William Dixie Hoxie (1866-1925), a marine engineer who patented a design for water-tube boiler, which Babock & Wilcox manufactured. The ship was operated by Stockard and scrapped in 1970 in Tacoma, Washington.

SS William G Lee

The Hull #2865, SS William G Lee was a Liberty cargo ship and launched on Thursday, June 15, 1944. The ship was named after William Granville Lee (1859-1929), a railroad worker who became President of the Brotherhood of Railroad Trainman 1909-28. In 1949, the ship was renamed Nadine and in 1969 it was converted to a container ship by South Atlantic, then scrapped in 1970 in Pugent Sound, Tacoma, Washington.

SS William L McLean

The Hull #2890, SS William L McLean was a Liberty cargo ship and launched on Wednesday, December 13, 1944. The ship was named after William Lippard McLean (1852-1931), who published the Philadelphia Evening Bulletin. The ship was operated by William J. Rountree and scrapped in 1964 in Portland, Oregon.

SS William W Seaton

The Hull #2892, SS William W Seaton was a Liberty cargo ship and launched on Friday, December 22, 1944. The ship was named after William Winston Seaton (1785-1866), co-owner of the National Intelligencer Newspaper in Washington, D.C. He was also an official Congressional House reporter. The ship was operated by WSA from 1945-1951; renamed Seamerchant by Colonial SS Corp in 1951; renamed Menites by Nueva Granada in 1953; renamed Tempo by Universal Mariners in 1963; was aground by typhoon in Taipei.

SS *William L Yancey*

The Hull #1056, SS William L Yancey was a Liberty cargo ship and launched on Sunday, July 25, 1943. This ship was named after William Lowndes Yancey (1814-1863), who was a Confederate States Senator from Alabama, Alabama Congressman; as well as a diplomat, orator, journalist, slave owner and southern politician urging southerners to secede from the Union. The ship was later operated by J. H. Winchester; renamed Eleni Stathatos by Anthony D Stathatos in 1947; sold to Seafarers Investments in 1961; renamed Cebollati by Gasmar in 1965; and was scrapped in 1969 in Shanghai.

SS William Black Yates

The Hull #1062, SS William Black Yates was a Liberty cargo ship and launched on Tuesday, September 7, 1943 and later operated by T. J. Stevenson. This ship was named after South Carolina Chaplain William Black Yates (1809-1882), who for 46 years served as chaplain of the Seamans bethel. The ship was operated by T. J. Stevenson and scrapped in 1970 in New York.

WWII Ships, Vessels & Their Namesakes of Savannah, Georgia
Coastal Cargo Ships 1945

The coastal cargo ships "C1-M-AVI" were advertised as 4,000-ton ships but designed to carry 6,000 tons, built by the Southeastern Shipbuilding Corporation. These were dry-cargo ships.

AV-1 Check Knot

The AV-1 Check Knot was a Coastal cargo ship and launched on Saturday, January 13, 1945. This ship was named after Sgt. Joseph E. Muller (1908-1945), a US Army soldier, recipient of the Medal of Honor for his actions in WWII and the Battle of Okinawa. The ship was transferred to the US Army and renamed USAT Sgt. Joseph E Muller, then to the Navy in 1950 to the Military Sea Transportation Service assigned to the Korean war. From 1962-1969 she worked under the Auxiliary General based out of Florida before being scrapped.

AV-2 Becket Bend

The AV-2 Becket Bend was a Coastal cargo ship and launched on Saturday, January 13, 1945. The ship was transferred from the War Shipping Administration to the Army in 1954 and renamed Private John F. Thoroson in 1947 until transferred to the Navy in 1950. The US Navy renamed the ship as USNS Private John F. Thorson T-AK-247 until 1954 and decommissioned. The Maritime Administration sold it to Hugo New Steel Productions in New York for scrap in 1960.

AV-3 Flemish Knot

The AV-3 Flemish Knot was a Coastal cargo ship and launched on Friday, February 9, 1945. The ship was scrapped in 1971.

AV-4 Snakehead

The AV-4 Snakehead was a Coastal cargo ship and launched on Saturday, February 24, 1945. The ship was sold privately in 1972 and converted to Drill ship Canmar Explorer.

AV-5 Link Splice

The AV-5 Link Splice was a Coastal cargo ship and launched on Saturday, March 17, 1945. The ship was renamed as Sgt. Jonah E Kelley, in 1947; then transferred to the US Navy as T-APC-116 in 1950 and scrapped in 1972.

AV-6 Diamond Hitch

The AV-6 Diamond Hitch was a Coastal cargo ship and launched on Saturday, March 17, 1945. The ship was used for American Export Lines in 1946 as a Reserve Fleet. Alaska SS Co bought it in 1949 to 1953. Olympic Steamship used it as Reserve Fleet in 1955 to 1956.

AV-7 Persian Knot

The AV-7 Persian Knot was a Coastal cargo ship and launched on Thursday, April 5, 1945, and was sold to Korea in 1956.

AV-8 Marline Bend

The AV-8 Marline Bend was a Coastal cargo ship and launched on Thursday, April 5, 1945. The ship was sold for scrap in 1970.

AV-9 Ring Hitch

The AV-9 Ring Hitch was a Coastal cargo ship and launched on Monday, April 23, 1945. The ship was sent to France as Canche and scrapped in 1969.

AV-10 Grass Knot

The AV-10 Grass Knot was a Coastal cargo ship and launched on Monday, April 30, 1945. The ship was sent to France as refrigerated cargo under the name of Bresle. It exploded and was abandoned in 1971.

AV-11 Sailmaker's Splice

The AV-11 Sailmaker's Splice was a Coastal cargo ship and launched on Monday, May 14, 1945. The ship was sent to Chile as Antartico.

AV-12 Long Eye

The AV-12 Long Eye was a Coastal cargo ship and launched on Wednesday, June 6, 1945. The ship was sent to Chile as the Almagro and sank in 1976.

AV-13 Crossing Knot

The AV-13 Crossing Knot was a Coastal cargo ship and launched on Tuesday, June 19, 1945.

AV-14 Solid Sinnet

The AV-14 Solid Sinnet was a Coastal cargo ship and launched on Saturday, June 30, 1945. The ship was sent to France as Dives and scrapped in 1967.

AV-15 Flat Knot

The AV-15 Flat Knot was a Coastal cargo ship and launched on Wednesday, July 11, 1945. The ship was sent to France as Aulne.

AV-16 Horseshoe Splice

The AV-16 Horseshoe Splice was a Coastal cargo ship and launched on Saturday, July 14, 1945. The ship was sent to France as Couesnon, scrapped in 1970.

AV-17 Double Loop

The AV-17 Double Loop was a Coastal cargo ship and launched on Thursday, September 6, 1945. The ship was sold privately in 1947.

AV-18 Half Knot

The AV-18 Half Knot was a Coastal cargo ship and launched on Friday, September 14, 1945. The ship was sold privately in 1948 and scrapped in 1973.

WWII Ships, Vessels & Their Namesakes of Savannah, Georgia
Naval Vessels 1942-1946

Savannah Machine and Foundry made naval minesweeping vessels for WWII usage.

The Savannah Machine & Foundry was founded in 1912 by Walter Lee Mingledorff, who sold it to Aegis Corp. in 1968, who sold it to Saylor Marine in 1984, who sold it to Intermarine USA in 1987, who sold it to Bernie Ebbers in 1999, who forfeited it to WorldCom when he went to jail in 2002, who then sold it to Palmer Johnson, who sold it to Global Ship Systems in 2004, who failed in 2007. It was finally sold in the bankruptcy court in 2010, for $10 million, to neighboring Colonial Terminals.

USS Gazelle

The AM-17, USS Gazelle, a US Navy Minesweeper, weighing in at 1,250d tons and launched on Sunday, January 10, 1943. She served in the Royal Navy under Operation Cleaver to clear German mines, making way for a squadron to lead light cruisers with four destroyers to return to Copenhagen taking control of German cruisers Prinz Eugen and Numberg after their surrender.

USS Gorgon

The AM-18, USS Gorgon, a Catherine-class US Navy Minesweeper, weighing in at 1,250d tons and launched on Sunday, January 24, 1943. It went to Britain in 1943 as J346 and returned in 1946, disposition is unknown at this time.

USS Grecian

The AM-19, USS Grecian, a US Navy Minesweeper, weighing in at 1,250d tons and launched on Wednesday, March 10, 1943. It went to Britain as BAM-19 in 1943 as J352 and returned in 1946, then went to Turkey in 1947 as Edincik (M 509), struck 1974.

USS Implicit

The AM-246, USS Implicit, a US Navy Minesweeper, weighing 850d tons, and launched on Monday, September 6, 1943. She worked minesweeping and patrolling in Algeria, southern France, Palermo, and the historic Yalta. She arrived at Pearl Harbor five days after the surrender of Japan. After the war, she went to South China, San Pedro, and the Hawaiian Islands before transferring to China in 1948 as Yung Chia, to Taiwan in 1949, struck in 1986.

USS Improve

The AM-247, USS Improve, a US Navy Minesweeper, weighing 850d tons, and launched on Monday, September 6, 1943 and was sponsored by Mrs. J. E. Poythress. She performed her minesweeping duties off Africa, southern France, southern Italy, then shifted to the Pacific. It was sold privately in 1949 and sunk in 1953.

USS Incessant

The AM-248, USS Incessant, a US Navy Minesweeper, weighing in at 850d tons, and launched on Friday, October 22, 1943 and sponsored by Mrs. Ralston Mingledorff. She was built to clear minefields in offshore waters on the Italian Riviera and the French coast, then began air-sea rescue work in the Black Sea. She was sent to Shanghai and was to transfer to China in 1943, sunk in Mayville, Kentucky in 1995.

USS Incredible

The AM-249, USS Incredible, a US Navy Minesweeper, weighing in at 850d tons, and launched on Sunday, November 21, 1943 and was sponsored by Mrs. Herbert Hezlep. She escorted a convoy to North Africa for southern France invasion, repelled an attack of human guided torpedoes, continued minesweeping in France and sailed to Russia and the Black Sea. She arrived eight days after the Japanese surrender at Pearl Harbor and continued to mine sweep and rescued survivors from the USS Pirate. Then she went to Japan, Korea and was finally scrapped in 1960.

USS Indicative

The AM-250, USS Indicative, a US Navy Minesweeper, weighing in at 850d tons, and launched Sunday, December 12, 1943. During WWII, she worked as a convoy escort protecting convoys from German submarines operating in western Atlantic Ocean. She went to USSR in 1945 as T 278, sunk off North Korea in 1945.

USS Inflict

The AM-251, USS Inflict, a US Navy minesweeper, weighing 850d tons, and launched on Sunday, January 16, 1944. She was built to clear minefields in offshore waters and performed exercises off the Virginia coast, and then for anti-submarine warfare exercises, then went to Okinawa operations. She was sold to Ricardo Granola and renamed Manabi and placed into mercantile service in 1948 and sunk in 1953.

USS Instill

The AM-252, USS Instill, a US Navy minesweeper, weighing 850d tons, and launched on Sunday, March 5, 1944. She was used for training in Guantanamo Bay, Cuba, used in the Korean War and minesweeping the east coast. She went to Mexico in 1962 as DM 10 and was struck in 1986.

USS Intrigue

The AM-253, USS Intrigue, a US Navy minesweeper, weighing in at 850d tons, and launched on Saturday, April 8, 1944. She was used in the Atlantic during WWII sailing with cargo ships to the Panama Canal and went as far as Newfoundland; then she went to Mexico in 1962 and was renamed Vicente Suarez (C61) and was stricken in 2001.

USS Invade

The AM-254, USS Invade, a US Navy minesweeper, weighing in at 850d tons, and launched on Sunday, February 6, 1944. She was used for the US Navy from 1944-1946, and the Mexican Navy from 1962 to 1994, being renamed as Ignaciao Zaragoza (C60) and is still active.

USS Kittiwake

The ASR-13, USS Kittiwake, a US Navy rescue salvage submarine, weighing in at 1,780d tons, and launched on Tuesday, July 10, 1945. From 1949 to 1965 she was used for accompanying and/or rescue duty to submarines from the Virgin Islands, Puerto Rico, Rota, Spain, Cuba, and the Caribbean. It was reefed in the Caymans in 2010.

USS Magic

The AM-20, USS Magic, a US Navy Minesweeper, weighing in at 1,250d tons, and launched on Monday, May 24, 1943. It went to Britain in 1943 as J400, hit by a human torpedo and was lost off Normandy in 1944.

USS Minivet

The AM-371, USS Minivet, a US Navy minesweeper, weighing in at 1,250d tons, and launched on Wednesday, November 8, 1944. She was used in training at Little Creek, Virginia, steamed out of Norfolk and went to the Far East – Japan, then to Pusan, Korea, Japan. She sank when she struck a mine in Japan and was lost at sea in 1945 losing 31 men.

USS Murrelet

The AMM-372, USS Murrelet, a US Navy minesweeper, weighing in at 1,250d tons, and launched on Friday, December 29, 1944. She was used for dangerous missions of removing mines from water minefields to allow ships to pass, and went to the Philippines in 1965 as Rizal (PS 74) and is currently active.

USS Peregrine

The AM-373, USS Peregrine, a US Navy minesweeper, weighing in at 1,250d tons, and launched on Tuesday, February 20, 1945. She was used for dangerous missions of removing mines from water minefields to then allow ships to pass and was reclassified as AG 176 in 1964 and struck in 1969.

USS Petrel

The ASR-14, USS Petrel, a US Navy rescue salvage submarine, weighing 1,780d tons, and launched on Wednesday, September 26, 1945. From 1946-1949, she was used to train and qualify deep-sea divers, salvage crews and escort submarines. From 1950-1959, she went to help divers extricate the battleship Missouri and aided submarine Guavina stranded in Key West. From 1960-1969 she was used for exercises off Portugal, Scotland and Israel. It was scrapped in 2003.

USS Pigeon

The AM-374, USS Pigeon, a US Navy minesweeper, weighing in at 1,250d tons, and launched on Wednesday, March 28, 1945. She was used for dangerous missions of removing mines from water minefields to then allow ships to pass and scrapped in 1967.

USS Pochard

The AM-375, USS Pochard, a US Navy minesweeper, weighed in at 1,250d tons, and launched on Sunday, June 11, 1944. She was used for dangerous missions of removing mines from water minefields to then allow ships to pass, and she was a heavy-bodied diving duck. It was scrapped in 1967.

USS Ptarmigan

The AM-376, USS Ptarmigan, a US Navy minesweeper, weighing in at 1,250d tons, and launched on Saturday, July 15, 1944. She was used for dangerous missions of removing mines from water minefields to then allow ships to pass. It went to Korea in 1963 as Shin Song (PCE 711) and was struck in 1984.

WWII Ships, Vessels & Their Namesakes of Savannah, Georgia

USS Pylades

The AM-21, USS Pylades, a US Navy Minesweeper, weighing in at 1,250d tons, and launched on Sunday, June 27, 1943 and sponsored by Mrs. Helen P. Page. It went to Britain in 1943 as J401, sunk by a midget submarine and was lost off Normandy in 1944.

USS Quail

The AM-377, USS Quail, a US Navy minesweeper, weighed 1,250d tons, and launched on Sunday, August 20, 1944 . She was used for dangerous missions of removing mines from water minefields to then allow ships to pass and was scrapped in 1967.

USS Redstart

The AM 378, USS Redstart, a US Navy minesweeper, weighing in at 1,205d tons, and launched on Wednesday, October 18, 1944. After WWII, she was used to mine sweep at the Panama Canal, and Pearl Harbor. She swept mines during the Korean War and after then went to Japan. It went to Taiwan in 1965 as Wu Sheng (PCE 884) and struck in 1998.

USS Sunbird

The ASR-15, USS Sunbird, a US Navy rescue salvage submarine, weighing in at 1,780d tons, and launched on Wednesday, April 3, 1946. From 1950-1959, she held sea trials at New London and even towed disabled submarines. From 1960-1969, she aided two tugs towing the decommissioned Chenango (CVHE-28). From 1970-1979, she was deployed to the Caribbean. From 1980-1993 she was used for search and recovery of debris and wreckage from the ill-fated Space Shuttle Challenger. It was scrapped in 2005.

USS Symbol

The AM 123, USS Symbol, a US Navy Minesweeper, weighing in at 1,250d tons and launched on Thursday, July 2, 1942, receiving five battle stars for WWII. It went to Mexico in 1972 as Guillermo Prieto (C71) and is still active. It received two battle stars for Korea.

USS Threat

The AM-124, USS Threat, a US Navy Minesweeper, weighing in at 1,250d tons and launched on Saturday, August 15, 1942. The minesweeper had convoy operations to North Africa in 1943, then to Europe in 1944, receiving three battle stars for WWII. It went to Mexico in 1973 as Francisco Zarco (C81).

WWII Ships, Vessels & Their Namesakes of Savannah, Georgia

USS Tide

The AM-125, USS Tide, a US Navy Minesweeper, weighing in at 1,250d tons and launched on September 7, 1942. It performed North African operations in 1943, stateside operations in late 1943, European operations in 1944. The ship struck a mine off Utah beach during Normandy and was lost at sea in 1944, receiving on battle star for WWII.

USS Tringa

The ASR-16, USS Tringa, a US Navy rescue salvage submarine, weighing in at 1,780d tons, and launched on Tuesday, Jun 25, 1948. She participated in several rescue experiments for the Bureau of Ships, testing diving bells, submarine buoys, ground tackle, mooring gear, and related equipment. She aided the Harder (SS-568) off the coast of Ireland, because the Harder broke down. From 1960-1970, she alternated deployments to the Mediterranean, underwent a series of overhauls and was mostly used for rescues. It was struck in 1977, to be sunk as target.

WWII Ships, Vessels & Their Namesakes of Savannah, Georgia
Concrete Barges 1943-1944

Typical WWII Concrete Fleet

The Macevoy Shipbuilding Company built concrete barges that played a crucial role in World War II operations, particularly during D-Day Normandy landings. They were used for fuel and munitions transportation, as block-ships and floating pontoons. They were launched on the following dates:

Concrete No. 6

Type B7-A1, MC # 619, launched on Tuesday, Jun 25, 1943.

Concrete No. 7

Type B7-A1, MC # 620, weighing in at 5,794d tons and launched on Monday, July 26, 1943 for the US Navy.

Concrete No. 8

Type B7-A1, MC # 621, launched on Monday, November 29, 1943

Concrete No. 9

Type B7-A1, MC # 622, launched on Tuesday, December 28, 1943

Concrete No. 10

Type B7-A1, MC # 623, launched on Sunday, April 9, 1944

Concrete No. 11

Type B7-A1, MC # 903, launched on Saturday, April 22, 1944

Concrete No. 12

Type B7-A1, MC # 904, launched on Sunday, May 21, 1944

Made in the USA
Columbia, SC
16 January 2025